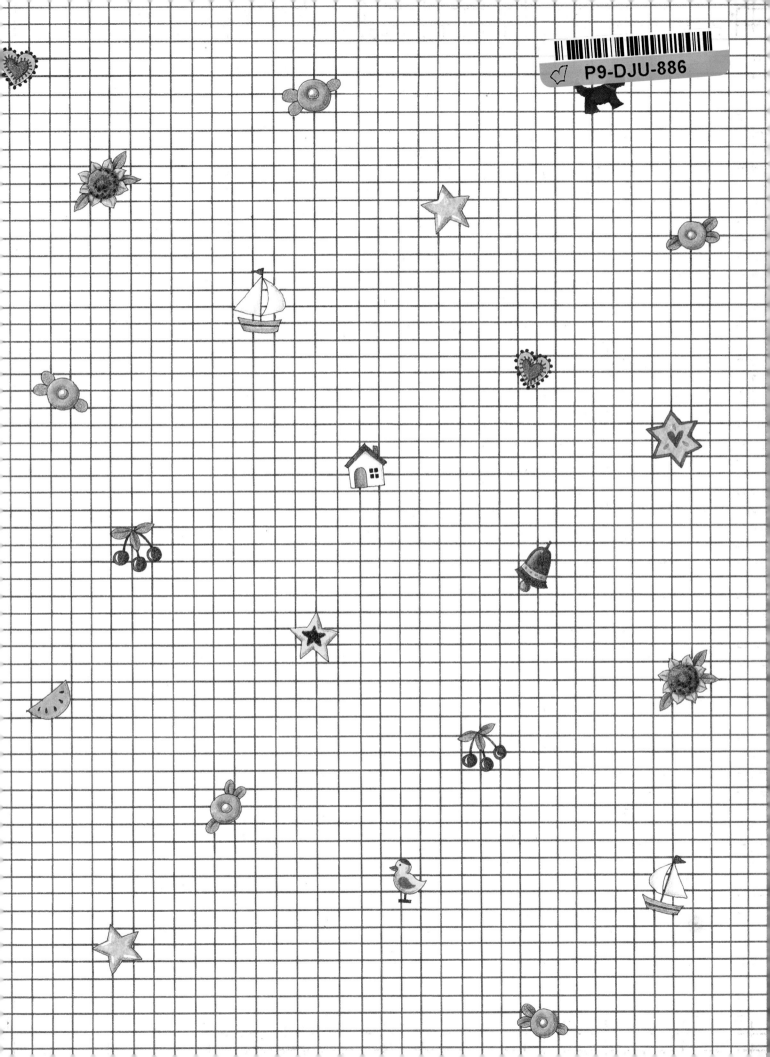

Christmas Journal

Illustrated by Mary Engelbreit

Written by Catherine Hoesterey

Andrews and McMeel
A Universal Press Syndicate Company
Kansas City

Christmas Journal © Mary Engelbreit Ink 1994.
All rights reserved. Printed in Singapore.
No part of this book may be used or reproduced in any manner whatsoever
without written permission except in the case of reprints in the context of reviews.
For information write
Andrews and McMeel, a Universal Press Syndicate Company
4900 Main Street, Kansas City, MO 64112.

ISBN: 0-8362-4623-3

Text design by Stephanie Raaf

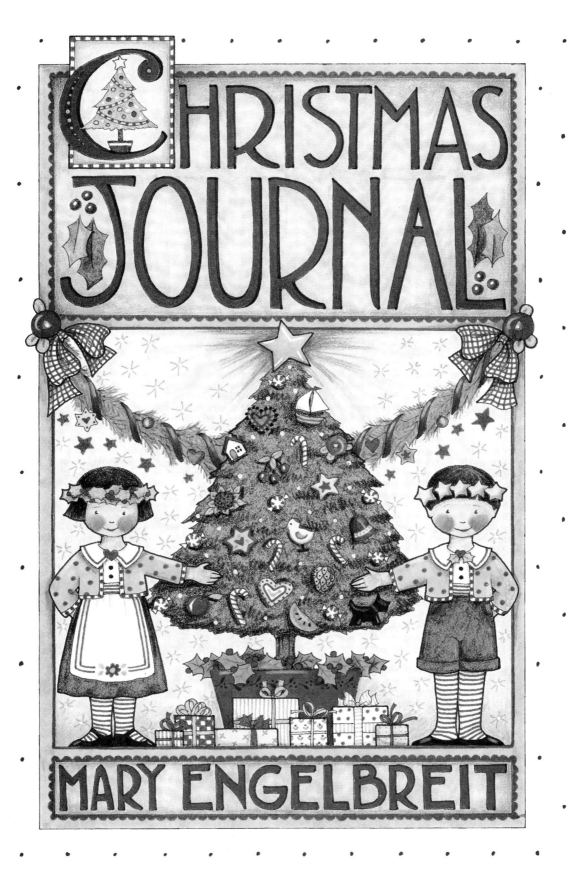

CHRISTMAS JOURNAL

MARY ENGELBREIT

Welcome to the Christmas Journal!

Christmas is the wide-eyed wonder of a child who believes. It's a surprise visit from a long-absent friend. Christmas is cookies baking, cozy fires burning, voices singing, bright lights twinkling, and the gathering of loved ones from far away. Christmas is a million sights and sounds and sensations. Christmas should be savored and honored for the miracle it performs every year—bringing out the best in people.

Because Christmas is a collection of so many different elements, it can also be simply overwhelming. All the singular joys that make the Christmas season unlike any other can easily be lost in the chaos. This Christmas Journal was designed to prevent this from happening. It will help you to prepare for, enjoy, and remember your Christmases better than ever before. Entrust your memories to this book's pages. Make them a permanent home for your family's traditions and remembrances of this most magical time of year.

Merry Christmas!

Mary Engelbreit

Contents

How to Use This Book

Think of your *Christmas Journal* as two books in one. The first part provides space for you to record your personal memories of holidays past. This section is filled with thought-starting questions designed to help you recall the funny, poignant, and irreplaceable remembrances of your own past Christmases and those of your parents.

The second part of the book is a five-year journal for you to write in during each Christmas season. You may want to consider storing this book with your Christmas decorations; then, when it's time to take them out each year, you can review past years' entries and begin your journaling for the current year. Keep the journal in a convenient location. If you like to write before going to sleep, put it on a bedside table. Also, consider leaving the journal out where family members can share in it and enjoy the cherished memories it safeguards. Invite others to add their stories and comments to your journal. It's especially a treat to see what children, with their unique perspective of Christmas, will write!

Although this journal will prompt you in certain directions and remind you to record specific events, remember that you are keeping this journal for yourself. Use it in the way that works best for you. If some sections don't apply to the way you celebrate the holidays, skip them and put your energy into other areas. There are too many "mandatory" Christmas responsibilities that weigh upon us. Don't make writing in this book one of them. Keep your journal informal and have fun with it. Take advantage of the ample free-writing space to express yourself. When writing, pretend you're having a lively conversation with a friend.

Don't skip over the seemingly trivial. A last-minute trip to the store for that small but perfectly inspired gift, a holiday baking misadventure, a humorous anecdote heard at a party—all of these things will help frame your memories and keep them distinct and alive. Remember to date entries as you go. Be specific.

If you do sometimes need a little extra motivation for journal keeping, consider this. Think about how exciting it would be to discover, hidden in your attic or basement, a journal kept by your parent or grandparent. A journal that details their favorite time of year and candidly discusses the people and events that were special to them. Think what a treasure that would be.

The time and love you put into this journal can make it a treasure too, for yourself and for your family in years to come.

Memories of Christmas Past

How My Parents Celebrated:

Some stories my mother has told me about the Christmas traditions in her family:

_____
_____
_____
_____
_____
_____
_____
_____

Some stories my father has told me about the Christmas traditions in his family:

_____
_____
_____
_____
_____
_____
_____
_____

Christmas traditions that have been passed on from my parents include:

_____
_____
_____
_____
_____
_____
_____
_____
_____
_____

My Childhood Christmases:

One of my earliest memories of Christmas is: _____

_____

_____

_____

_____

_____

_____

_____

_____

_____

_____

Each family has its own unique traditions at Christmas. Some unusual Christmas customs in our family were: _____

_____

_____

_____

_____

_____

_____

_____

_____

_____

_____

Some enduring memories of my brothers and sisters or other close friends at Christmas include: _____

_____

_____

_____

_____

_____

_____

_____

_____

_____

To prepare for Christmas, our family would: _____
_____
_____
_____
_____
_____
_____
_____

Special Christmas decorations in our house included: _____
_____
_____
_____
_____
_____
_____
_____
_____
_____

An annual Christmas outing that was always a highlight was: _____
_____
_____
_____
_____
_____
_____
_____
_____
_____

A special Christmas event in our community was: _____
_____
_____
_____
_____
_____
_____

Some of my fondest memories of Christmas as a child are:

Favorite Christmas stories or songs from my childhood:

Memories of my school Christmas pageants and performances:

Some of my favorite Christmas presents ever were:

The biggest surprise I ever got at Christmas was:

As a child, the best present I ever gave to someone was:

My favorite Christmas treat to eat as a kid was:

Christmas homecomings or surprise visits I remember:

Celebrating Christmas Eve and Christmas Day:

Christmas Eve traditions in my family included: _____

_____

_____

_____

_____

_____

_____

_____

_____

_____

_____

_____

_____

_____

_____

_____

What Christmas morning and Christmas day were like at our house: _____

_____

_____

_____

_____

_____

_____

_____

_____

_____

_____

_____

_____

_____

_____

_____

_____

Holiday religious services we participated in: _____

_____

_____

_____

_____

_____

_____

_____

_____

_____

New Year's traditions: _____

_____

_____

_____

_____

_____

_____

_____

_____

_____

_____

_____

_____

My favorite New Year's memory: _____

_____

_____

_____

_____

_____

_____

_____

_____

_____

_____

_____

Ornaments & Decorations

Use this section to list Christmas ornaments and decorations that have special significance to you. If you can recall the history of a particular ornament or decoration, record it here.

Ornaments:

_____

_____

_____

_____

_____

_____

_____

_____

_____

_____

_____

_____

_____

_____

_____

_____

_____

_____

_____

_____

_____

_____

_____

_____

_____

_____

_____

Decorations and Collections:

Favorite Holiday Photographs

Attach favorite photographs from past holiday gatherings on these pages.

Favorite Holiday Photographs

Favorite Holiday Photographs

Favorite Holiday Recipes

IT IS A FINE SEASONING
FOR JOY TO THINK
OF THOSE WE LOVE.
·MOLIERE·

Favorite Holiday Recipes

Favorite Holiday Recipes

Master Christmas Card List

Name

Address

Name

Address

HE'S MAKING A LIST

HE'S CHECKING IT TWICE!

Master Christmas Card List

Name _____

Address _____

_____

_____

_____

_____

_____

_____

_____

_____

_____

_____

_____

_____

_____

_____

_____

_____

_____

_____

_____

_____

_____

_____

Name

Address

Master Christmas Card List

Name
Address

Name

Address

Year One

Preparations for the Season

Use this section to record your progress in preparing for the arrival of the holidays.

Year of journal _____

Date Christmas journaling begun _____

Summary of my holiday planning status on this date: _____

_____
_____
_____
_____
_____
_____
_____
_____
_____

Goals for this holiday season: _____

_____
_____
_____
_____
_____
_____
_____
_____
_____
_____
_____
_____

Additions to Christmas Card List

Christmas Card List:

Name

Address

Holiday Planning Calendar

Parties, programs, performances, appointments, mail-ordering deadlines, etc.

Sun	Mon	Tues	Wed	Thurs	Fri	Sat

Decking the Halls:

Lights, greenery, nativity scenes, candles, stockings, indoor and outdoor decorations.

Trimming the Tree:

New ornaments, heirloom decorations, type of tree.

Getting into the Spirit of Christmas:

Tasks to Remember:

Have family picture taken for Christmas card

Begin work on family newsletter

Purchase Christmas cards early

Gather catalogs

Leave ample time to finish homemade or handmade presents

Begin baking early

Notes:

Seasonal Fun

Use this section to report on all the fun activities of the season.

Outings and Activities:

Ice-skating, sledding, Christmas tree hunting, trips to Santa, concerts, home-tours, ballet, opera, etc.

Events:

School programs, lighting ceremonies, community events, etc.

Parties:

Dinners, caroling parties, company parties, etc.

Additional comments:

Celebrating Christmas

Use this section to write about the people and events that made your Christmas special this year.

Family fun: _____
_____
_____
_____
_____
_____
_____

Surprises: _____
_____
_____
_____
_____
_____
_____
_____

Homecomings and guests: _____
_____
_____
_____
_____
_____

Great gifts: _____
_____
_____
_____
_____
_____
_____

Travel:

Great goofs and near-calamities:

My favorite Christmas moment this year:

Something (or someone) that made this year extra special:

Additional thoughts:

Wrapping Up & Looking Ahead

Use this section for your post-holiday wrap-up. Record things to remember from this year that will make your holidays smoother and more enjoyable next year.

Special gifts, cards, or kindnesses received:

_____
_____
_____
_____
_____
_____
_____
_____

My favorite thing about the holidays this year:

_____
_____
_____
_____
_____
_____
_____

New additions to ornament or other collections:

_____
_____
_____
_____
_____
_____

An unexpected occurrence this holiday season: _____
_____
_____
_____
_____
_____
_____
_____
_____

Things I want to remember for next year: _____
_____
_____
_____
_____
_____
_____
_____
_____
_____
_____

Additional comments: _____
_____
_____
_____
_____
_____
_____

Date *Christmas Journal* put away for the year: _____

Year Two

Preparations for the Season

Use this section to record your progress in preparing for the arrival of the holidays.

Year of journal _____

Date Christmas journaling begun _____

Summary of my holiday planning status on this date: _____

_____

_____

_____

_____

_____

_____

_____

_____

_____

_____

Goals for this holiday season: _____

_____

_____

_____

_____

_____

_____

_____

_____

_____

_____

_____

_____

Additions to Christmas Card List

Christmas Card List:

Name _____

Address _____

_____

_____

_____

_____

_____

_____

_____

_____

_____

_____

_____

_____

_____

_____

_____

_____

_____

_____

_____

Holiday Planning Calendar

Parties, programs, performances, appointments, mail-ordering deadlines, etc.

Sun	Mon	Tues	Wed	Thurs	Fri	Sat

Decking the Halls:

Lights, greenery, nativity scenes, candles, stockings, indoor and outdoor decorations.

Trimming the Tree:

New ornaments, heirloom decorations, type of tree.

Getting into the Spirit of Christmas:

Tasks to Remember:

- Have family picture taken for Christmas card
- Begin work on family newsletter
- Purchase Christmas cards early
- Gather catalogs
- Leave ample time to finish homemade or handmade presents
- Begin baking early
- Notes:

Seasonal Fun

Use this section to report on all the fun activities of the season.

Outings and Activities:
Ice-skating, sledding, Christmas tree hunting, trips to Santa, concerts, home-tours, ballet, opera, etc.

Events:
School programs, lighting ceremonies, community events, etc.

Parties:
Dinners, caroling parties, company parties, etc.

Additional comments:

Celebrating Christmas

Use this section to write about the people and events that made your Christmas special this year.

Family fun:

Surprises:

Homecomings and guests:

Great gifts:

Travel:

Great goofs and near-calamities:

My favorite Christmas moment this year:

Something (or someone) that made this year extra special:

Additional thoughts:

Wrapping Up & Looking Ahead

Use this section for your post-holiday wrap-up. Record things to remember from this year that will make your holidays smoother and more enjoyable next year.

Special gifts, cards, or kindnesses received:

My favorite thing about the holidays this year:

New additions to ornament or other collections:

An unexpected occurrence this holiday season:

_____
_____
_____
_____
_____
_____
_____
_____
_____

Things I want to remember for next year:

_____
_____
_____
_____
_____
_____
_____
_____
_____
_____

Additional comments:

_____
_____
_____
_____
_____
_____
_____

Date *Christmas Journal* put away for the year: _____

Year Three

Preparations for the Season

Use this section to record your progress in preparing for the arrival of the holidays.

Year of journal _____

Date Christmas journaling begun _____

Summary of my holiday planning status on this date:

_____
_____
_____
_____
_____
_____
_____
_____
_____
_____
_____
_____

Goals for this holiday season:

_____
_____
_____
_____
_____
_____
_____
_____
_____
_____
_____
_____
_____
_____
_____
_____

Additions to Christmas Card List

Christmas Card List:

Name _____

Address _____

Holiday Planning Calendar

Parties, programs, performances, appointments, mail-ordering deadlines, etc.

Sun	Mon	Tues	Wed	Thurs	Fri	Sat

Decking the Halls:

Lights, greenery, nativity scenes, candles, stockings, indoor and outdoor decorations.

Trimming the Tree:

New ornaments, heirloom decorations, type of tree.

AN INTIMATE VIEW OF CHRISTMAS

Getting into the Spirit of Christmas:

_____
_____
_____
_____
_____
_____
_____
_____
_____
_____
_____
_____
_____

Tasks to Remember:

- Have family picture taken for Christmas card
- Begin work on family newsletter
- Purchase Christmas cards early
- Gather catalogs
- Leave ample time to finish homemade or handmade presents
- Begin baking early
- Notes: _____

_____
_____
_____
_____
_____
_____
_____
_____
_____

Seasonal Fun

Use this section to report on all the fun activities of the season.

Outings and Activities:
Ice-skating, sledding, Christmas tree hunting, trips to Santa, concerts, home-tours, ballet, opera, etc.

Events:
School programs, lighting ceremonies, community events, etc.

Parties:

Dinners, caroling parties, company parties, etc.

Additional comments:

HARK! HAROLD
♥ THE ANGEL ♥
SINGS

Celebrating Christmas

Use this section to write about the people and events that made your Christmas special this year.

Family fun:

_____
_____
_____
_____
_____

Surprises:

_____
_____
_____
_____
_____
_____
_____

Homecomings and guests:

_____
_____
_____
_____
_____
_____

Great gifts:

_____
_____
_____
_____
_____
_____

Travel:

Great goofs and near-calamities:

My favorite Christmas moment this year:

Something (or someone) that made this year extra special:

Additional thoughts:

Wrapping Up & Looking Ahead

Use this section for your post-holiday wrap-up. Record things to remember from this year that will make your holidays smoother and more enjoyable next year.

Special gifts, cards, or kindnesses received:

My favorite thing about the holidays this year:

New additions to ornament or other collections:

An unexpected occurrence this holiday season: _____

_____

_____

_____

_____

_____

_____

_____

_____

_____

Things I want to remember for next year: _____

_____

_____

_____

_____

_____

_____

_____

_____

_____

Additional comments: _____

_____

_____

_____

_____

_____

_____

Date *Christmas Journal* put away for the year: _____

Year Four

Preparations for the Season

Use this section to record your progress in preparing for the arrival of the holidays.

Year of journal _____

Date Christmas journaling begun _____

Summary of my holiday planning status on this date: _____

_____

_____

_____

_____

_____

_____

_____

_____

Goals for this holiday season: _____

_____

_____

_____

_____

_____

_____

_____

_____

_____

_____

Additions to Christmas Card List

Christmas Card List:

Name _____

Address _____

Holiday Planning Calendar

Parties, programs, performances, appointments, mail-ordering deadlines, etc.

Sun	Mon	Tues	Wed	Thurs	Fri	Sat

Decking the Halls:

Lights, greenery, nativity scenes, candles, stockings, indoor and outdoor decorations.

Trimming the Tree:

New ornaments, heirloom decorations, type of tree.

Getting into the Spirit of Christmas:

Tasks to Remember:

Have family picture taken for Christmas card

Begin work on family newsletter

Purchase Christmas cards early

Gather catalogs

Leave ample time to finish homemade or handmade presents

Begin baking early

Notes:

Seasonal Fun

Use this section to report on all the fun activities of the season.

Outings and Activities:
Ice-skating, sledding, Christmas tree hunting, trips to Santa, concerts, home-tours, ballet, opera, etc.

Events:
School programs, lighting ceremonies, community events, etc.

Parties:

Dinners, caroling parties, company parties, etc.

_____

_____

_____

_____

_____

_____

_____

_____

_____

_____

_____

_____

_____

Additional comments: _____

_____

_____

_____

_____

_____

_____

_____

_____

_____

Celebrating Christmas

Use this section to write about the people and events that made your Christmas special this year.

Family fun:

Surprises:

Homecomings and guests:

Great gifts:

Travel:

Great goofs and near-calamities:

My favorite Christmas moment this year:

Something (or someone) that made this year extra special:

Additional thoughts:

Wrapping Up & Looking Ahead

Use this section for your post-holiday wrap-up. Record things to remember from this year that will make your holidays smoother and more enjoyable next year.

Special gifts, cards, or kindnesses received:

_____

_____

_____

_____

_____

_____

_____

My favorite thing about the holidays this year:

_____

_____

_____

_____

_____

_____

_____

_____

New additions to ornament or other collections:

_____

_____

_____

_____

_____

An unexpected occurrence this holiday season:

Things I want to remember for next year:

Additional comments:

Date *Christmas Journal* put away for the year:

Year Five

Preparations for the Season

Use this section to record your progress in preparing for the arrival of the holidays.

Year of journal

Date Christmas journaling begun

Summary of my holiday planning status on this date:

Goals for this holiday season:

Additions to Christmas Card List

Christmas Card List:

Name

Address

Holiday Planning Calendar

Parties, programs, performances, appointments, mail-ordering deadlines, etc.

Sun	Mon	Tues	Wed	Thurs	Fri	Sat

Decking the Halls:

Lights, greenery, nativity scenes, candles, stockings, indoor and outdoor decorations.

Trimming the Tree:

New ornaments, heirloom decorations, type of tree.

Getting into the Spirit of Christmas:

Tasks to Remember:

Have family picture taken for Christmas card

Begin work on family newsletter

Purchase Christmas cards early

Gather catalogs

Leave ample time to finish homemade or handmade presents

Begin baking early

Notes:

Seasonal Fun

Use this section to report on all the fun activities of the season.

Outings and Activities:
Ice-skating, sledding, Christmas tree hunting, trips to Santa, concerts, home-tours, ballet, opera, etc.

Events:
School programs, lighting ceremonies, community events, etc.

Parties:

Dinners, caroling parties, company parties, etc.

Additional comments:

The CHRISTMAS PAGEANT

Celebrating Christmas

Use this section to write about the people and events that made your Christmas special this year.

Family fun: _____
_____
_____
_____
_____
_____

Surprises: _____
_____
_____
_____
_____
_____
_____

Homecomings and guests: _____
_____
_____
_____
_____
_____

Great gifts: _____
_____
_____
_____
_____
_____

Travel:

Great goofs and near-calamities:

My favorite Christmas moment this year:

Something (or someone) that made this year extra special:

Additional thoughts:

Wrapping Up & Looking Ahead

Use this section for your post-holiday wrap-up. Record things to remember from this year that will make your holidays smoother and more enjoyable next year.

Special gifts, cards, or kindnesses received:

My favorite thing about the holidays this year:

New additions to ornament or other collections:

An unexpected occurrence this holiday season:

Things I want to remember for next year:

Additional comments:

Date *Christmas Journal* put away for the year:

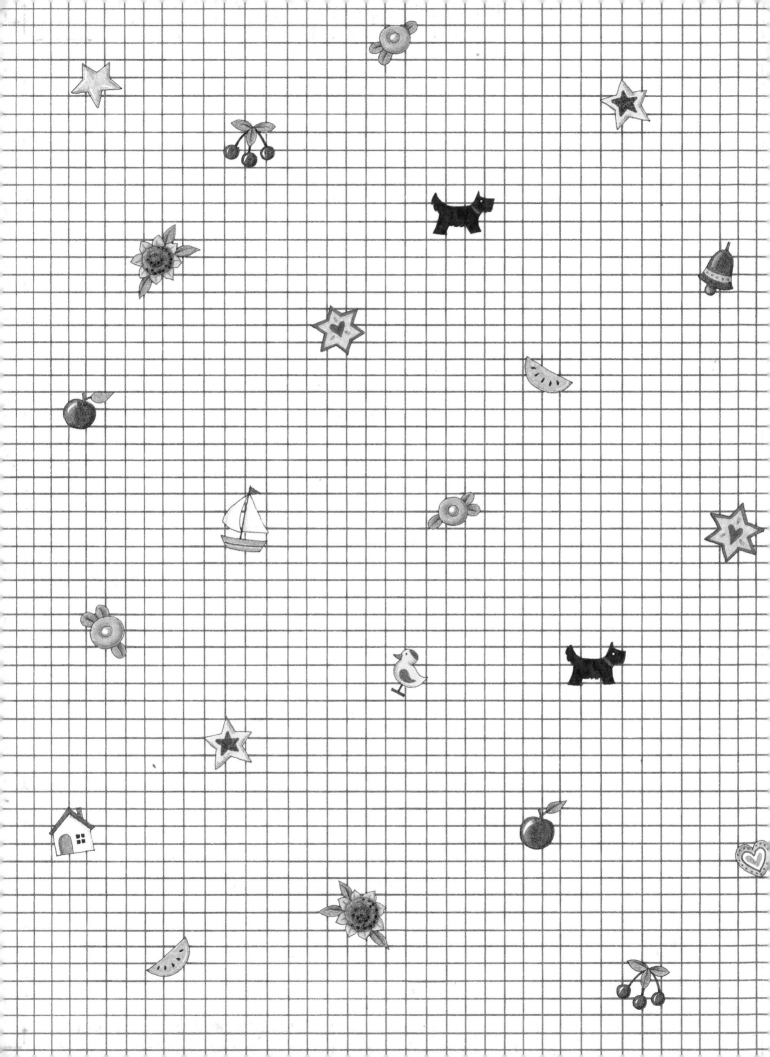